BEAUTIFUL CREATURES

DAD ISN'T COMING OUT TO EAT AGAIN... HE WRITES ALL NIGHT AND SLEEPS ALL DAY. IT'S BEEN THAT WAY SINCE MY MOM DIED LAST APRIL.

HONK HONK

OH, LINK'S HERE.

WHAT DO YOU THINK OF MY BAND'S NEW TRACK?

I THINK IT NEEDS WORK. LIKE ALL YOUR SONGS.

YEAH? WELL, YOUR FACE NEEDS WORK.

VRMMMM

LINK AND I HAVE BEEN BEST FRIENDS EVER SINCE HE GAVE ME HALF OF HIS TWINKIE ON THE BUS TO KINDERGARTEN.

I ONLY FOUND OUT LATER IT HAD FALLEN ON THE FLOOR...

LINK'S BAND IS A TRAGEDY. BUT AT LEAST HE KNOWS WHAT HE WANTS TO DO.

ALL I HAVE IS A SHOEBOX FULL OF COLLEGE BROCHURES. I DON'T CARE WHERE I GO, SO LONG AS IT'S A THOUSAND MILES FROM GATLIN. MY DAD SAYS THERE ARE ONLY TWO KINDS OF PEOPLE IN THIS TOWN—THE ONES WHO ARE BOUND TO STAY OR TOO DUMB TO GO. EVERYONE ELSE FINDS A WAY OUT.

I READ ALL THE TIME. BUT I KEEP THAT TO MYSELF. AROUND HERE BOOKS AND BASKETBALL DON'T MIX. WHAT WOULD THE TEAM, MY FRIENDS, SAY IF THEY KNEW?

The War of Northern Aggression

DON'T YOU MEAN THE CIVIL WAR?

GATLIN, SOUTH CAROLINA, ISN'T LIKE THE SMALL TOWNS YOU SEE IN THE MOVIES. UNLESS IT'S A MOVIE FROM FIFTY YEARS AGO.

IN GATLIN, THE FIRST DAY OF SCHOOL NEVER CHANGES. THE TEACHERS DECIDED IF YOU WERE STUPID OR SMART BACK IN KINDERGARTEN. I'M SMART BECAUSE MY PARENTS WERE PROFESSORS. LINK IS STUPID BECAUSE HE THREW UP DURING THE CHRISTMAS PAGEANT.

...CHEMISTRY WASN'T MUCH BETTER. MR. HOLLENBACK DOOMED ME TO BE LAB PARTNERS WITH EMILY. MY EX...

THAT SUCKS.

BUT DID YOU HEAR? THERE'S A NEW GIRL IN OUR CLASS.

JACKSON HIGH

A NEW GIRL? IN *THIS* TOWN?

I WONDER IF SHE'S HOT. ♥

SO, Y'ALL HEARD ABOUT THE NEW GIRL?

IS SHE HOT? YOU GONNA PUT HER ON THE CHEERING SQUAD?

HARDLY! YOU SHOULD SEE WHAT SHE'S WEARIN'.

HEY, SAVANNAH.

EMILY.

STRIKE 1

AND HOW PALE SHE IS.

STRIKE 2

SAVANNAH SNOW. THE STANDARD BY WHICH ALL OTHER GIRLS AT JACKSON HIGH ARE MEASURED.

AND DO YOU KNOW WHO SHE IS? SHE'S OLD MAN RAVENWOOD'S NIECE!

STRIKE 3

MACON MELCHIZEDEK RAVENWOOD IS THE TOWN SHUT-IN. I DON'T THINK ANYONE IN TOWN HAS SEEN HIM SINCE BEFORE I WAS BORN. I REMEMBER ENOUGH OF *TO KILL A MOCKINGBIRD* TO KNOW OLD MAN RAVENWOOD MAKES BOO RADLEY LOOK LIKE A SOCIAL BUTTERFLY.

GASP!

A RAVENWOOD? DAMMIT!

?

THERE SHE IS!

THE POSSIBILITY OF MY DREAM GIRL SHOWING UP IN GATLIN DISAPPEARS BEFORE I CAN EVEN IMAGINE OUR FIRST DATE.

I'M DOOMED TO THREE MORE YEARS OF EMILYS.

TMP

TMP
TMP
TMP

AND THEN, THERE SHE WAS AGAIN. IN MY ENGLISH CLASS.

STARE

WHISPER

MUTTER

To Kill a Mockingbird

156

Glance

ACK! SHE CAUGHT ME STARING...

HERE, MS. DUCHANNES. WE'VE BEEN READING *TO KILL A MOCKINGBIRD*.

OH.

I HAVE MY OWN COPY. IT'S ONE OF MY FAVORITE BOOKS.

SHE READS. IT'S ONE OF HER FAVORITES? SHE JUST SAID IT, LIKE IT'S NORMAL.

WHOOPS~!

DO AS I SAY. TAKE THAT BACK WHERE YOU FOUND IT AND BURY IT. THEN YOU COME RIGHT HOME.

I DON'T WANT YOU MESSIN' WITH THAT DUCHANNES GIRL ANYMORE, YOU HEAR ME?

I SPENT TWO HOURS WANDERING AROUND SO AMMA WOULD BELIEVE I'D GONE BACK TO BURY THE LOCKET.

WE GOT TRUBS.

WHAT'D YOU HEAR?

JACKSON HIGH'S GOT ITSELF A REGULAR LYNCH MOB THIS MORNIN'. BEEN GOIN' ON SINCE FRIDAY NIGHT. I HEARD MY MOM TALKIN'.

MY MOM, EMILY'S MOM, SAVANNAH'S...THEY'VE BEEN BURNIN' UP THE PHONE LINES. OVERHEARD MY MOM TALKIN' ABOUT THE WINDOW BREAKIN' IN ENGLISH AND HOW SHE HEARD OLD MAN RAVENWOOD'S NIECE HAD BLOOD ON HER HANDS.

IN MY POCKET. WHEN AMMA SAW IT, HER EYES ALMOST FELL OUT OF HER HEAD, LIKE IT WAS TRIPLE HEXED.

BUT I FOUND OUT SOME THINGS FROM MY GREAT-GREAT AUNTS THIS WEEKEND. THE INITIALS ON THE LOCKET, ECW, STAND FOR ETHAN CARTER WATE. HE WAS MY GREAT-GREAT-GREAT-GREAT UNCLE.

THEY SAY I WAS NAMED AFTER HIM.

AND THE INITIALS GKD? IT'S GENEVIEVE, RIGHT?

THEY DIDN'T KNOW, BUT IT HAS TO BE. AND THE "D" MUST BE FOR DUCHANNES.

YOU SHOULD ASK YOUR UNCLE.

NO. MY UNCLE WON'T KNOW ANYTHING.

VRMᵐᵐ-

WOOF

RAVENWOOD'S DOG!!

GRRR

......!!

WILD DOGS CARRY RABIES. SOMEONE SHOULD NOTIFY THE COUNTY.

MRS. LINCOLN?!

PRINCIPAL HARPER WAS JUST TELLIN' ME HE'S PLANNIN' ON OFFERIN' THAT RAVEN-WOOD GIRL A TRANSFER. SHE CAN TAKE HER PICK OF ANY SCHOOL. AS LONG AS IT'S NOT JACKSON.

GRRR..

IT'S OUR RESPONSIBILITY, ETHAN. WE HAVE TO KEEP THE YOUNG PEOPLE IN THIS TOWN SAFE. AND AWAY FROM THE WRONG SORTA PEOPLE.

WHICH MEANS ANYONE WHO ISN'T LIKE YOU?

I'M SURE YOU UNDERSTAND MY MEANIN'. AFTER ALL, YOU'RE ONE OF US. YOUR DADDY WAS BORN HERE AND YOUR MAMMA WAS BURIED HERE. YOU BELONG HERE. NOT *EVERYONE* DOES.

GRRROWL

ONCE I GOT TO CLASS, THE DAY BECAME ABNORMALLY NORMAL.

THAT IS...UNTIL LINK DROPPED ME OFF AFTER BASKETBALL PRACTICE AND I DECIDED TO DO SOMETHING COMPLETELY INSANE.

I LIED TO AMMA. I TOLD HER I WAS GOING TO THE LIBRARY TO VISIT MARIAN, A FAMILY FRIEND, AND TO WORK ON A PROJECT, BUT...

...NOW I'M BACK AT RAVENWOOD MANOR.

THIS IS INSANE.

I SHOULDN'T DO THIS.

WHAT AM I DOING?!

!!

BARK

WOOF

GRRROWL

BARK

BUT I HAVE A FEELING LENA'S UNCLE MIGHT KNOW SOMETHING THAT COULD HELP US...

TELL HIM YOU DON'T WANT TO STAY!

TRUST ME, I DON'T.

TMP

W... WOW.

ETHAN. ......? ETHAN, COME ON.

COME DOWN, OR I'M COMING UP.

IF AMMA SAW LENA IN HER PAJAMAS IN OUR FRONT YARD IN THE MIDDLE OF THE NIGHT, SHE'D HAVE A HEART ATTACK...AND THEN A STROKE.

......

TMP

I WAS TOO SCARED TO TELL YOU... BUT NOW I'M TOO SCARED NOT TO TELL YOU...

WHATEVER IT IS, YOU CAN TELL ME. I KNOW WHAT IT'S LIKE TO HAVE A CRAZY FAMILY.

......

......

THE PEOPLE IN MY FAMILY, AND ME. WE HAVE... *POWERS.* WE CAN DO THINGS THAT REGULAR PEOPLE CAN'T DO. WE'RE BORN THAT WAY, WE CAN'T HELP IT. WE ARE WHAT WE ARE.

=sigh=

YOU HAVE NO IDEA.

IS SHE TALKING ABOUT...?

MAGIC

I'M AFRAID TO ASK.

AND WHAT, EXACTLY, ARE YOU?

CASTERS, LIKE, SPELLCASTERS.

LIKE, WITCHES?

ETHAN, DON'T BE RIDICULOUS.

Phew!

THAT'S JUST A DUMB STEREOTYPE.

LIKE JOCKS.

WHA-?

I TOLD LENA IT WAS NO BIG DEAL THAT SHE WAS— WHAT? A WITCH? A CASTER?

YEAH, NO BIG DEAL.

I'M A BIG LIAR.

SKRT

BUT EVER SINCE THEN, I ONLY EVER WANT TO BE WITH LENA.

SHE ISN'T MY GIRLFRIEND, I DON'T EVEN KNOW HOW SHE FEELS ABOUT ME. WE DON'T DATE. BUT I WANT TO.

IT DIDN'T TAKE LONG FOR WORD TO GET OUT THAT "OLD MAN RAVENWOOD'S NIECE" WAS HANGING OUT WITH "ETHAN WATE WHOSE MAMMA DIED JUST LAST YEAR."

STOP & SHOP

SHDING

NO WAY!

HUH?

WHAT?

I DON'T KNOW
WHAT HAPPENED.

ON THE WAY TO RAVENWOOD,
I JUST STARTED TALKING, UNTIL
I HAD TOLD RIDLEY THINGS I'D
NEVER TOLD ANYONE.

I TOLD HER ABOUT MY MOM,
ABOUT HOW SHE DIED.

I TOLD HER ABOUT AMMA,
ABOUT HOW SHE READS CARDS.

I TOLD HER ABOUT MY DAD, ABOUT
HOW HE'S HOLED UP IN HIS STUDY.

IT WAS
ALMOST LIKE
SHE WAS
SUCKING IT
OUT OF ME.

LARKIN! STOP THAT!

HIS... ARM...

GEEZ. JUST TRYIN' TO LIFT THE MOOD.

RIDLEY, THAT'S ENOUGH.

I SPENT JUST AS MUCH TIME WITH YOU AS LENA DID, UNCLE M. HOW DID SHE BECOME YOUR FAVORITE?

SO, CUZ, ANY BIG PLANS FOR YOUR BIRTHDAY?

YOU HAVE BEEN CLAIMED. IT'S OUT OF MY HANDS.

CLAIMED?

DIZZY...

SQUEEZE

IN A FEW MONTHS, YOU COULD END UP EXACTLY LIKE ME, LENA. DON'T YOU THINK BOYFRIEND HERE DESERVES TO KNOW EVERYTHING? THAT YOU HAVE NO IDEA IF YOU'RE LIGHT OR DARK? THAT YOU HAVE NO CHOICE?

SHUT UP!

I'M SO COLD... EVERYTHING'S FROZEN...

CHAPTER 3

FLINCH

WHERE AM I?

open your eyes

moments bleed together
no span to time

illuminate

Fate decides

until challenged by the Fated.

WHAT HAPPENED?

ETHAN!

ZZ—!

ARE YOU OKAY? RIDLEY WOULDN'T LET GO OF YOU, AND I DIDN'T KNOW WHAT TO DO.

SHFF

CREAK

YOU LOOKED LIKE YOU WERE IN SO MUCH PAIN, I JUST REACTED.

YOU MEAN THAT TORNADO IN THE MIDDLE OF YOUR HOUSE?

THAT'S WHAT HAPPENS. I GET ANGRY OR SCARED AND THEN... THINGS JUST HAPPEN.

JOLT

THINGS LIKE WINDOWS BREAKING?

WE'LL FIGURE SOMETHING OUT.

AFTER LEAVING RAVENWOOD MANOR, ALL I WANT IS TO RETURN TO LENA.

THMP

TMP TMP TMP

UGH, I CAN'T SLEEP.

WHAT?

SNEAK

WHERE IS AMMA GOING IN THE MIDDLE OF THE NIGHT?

CRRRK

NONSENSE. I RAISED THAT CHILD. DON'T YOU THINK I'D KNOW IT IF HE HAD ANY KIND OF POWER?

YOU'RE WRONG THIS TIME. I'M WARNING YOU, THERE IS MORE TO THE BOY THAN EITHER OF US REALIZED.

VRRMMM

I HEARD YOU LIKE DONUTS. I COULD HEAR YOUR STOMACH GROWLING ALL THE WAY FROM RAVENWOOD.

I'VE NEVER SEEN HER SO HAPPY... SHE DOESN'T KNOW ABOUT MACON AND AMMA. BUT I HAVE TO TELL HER.

NO NUMBER ON HER HAND TODAY. HER BIRTHDAY... 120 DAYS...

THAT DOESN'T MAKE ANY SENSE. WHY IS HE MEETING AMMA IN THE MIDDLE OF THE NIGHT TO TELL HER WE HAVE THE LOCKET?

WHY DON'T THEY WANT US TO HAVE IT? THERE'S SOMETHING THEY DON'T WANT US TO KNOW.

WE NEED TO FIND OUT WHAT HAPPENS NEXT.

BURNING A HOUSE WITH WOMEN IN IT.

IT CAN'T BE TRUE!

WHAT THE—?

JUST TAKE US TO THE CASTER LIBRARY, AND WE'LL FIGURE IT OUT OURSELVES.

......

ALL RIGHT. I'LL TAKE YOU THE NEXT TIME IT'S OPEN. THE CASTER LIBRARY'S HOURS ARE A BIT... IRREGULAR.

OF COURSE THEY ARE.

THE ONLY DAYS OF THE YEAR THAT THE GATLIN LIBRARY IS CLOSED ARE BANK HOLIDAYS.

SO THOSE ARE THE ONLY DAYS THE GATLIN CASTER LIBRARY IS OPEN.

HAPPY HALLOWEEN!

I DON'T CARE.

I CAN HANDLE THIS.

WHATEVER HAPPENS TO YOU, HAPPENS TO ME.

hol

THEY REALLY HATE ME...

They Really Hate You

Yes They Do!

HAHA

HEY, DO YOU HAVE ANY MAKEUP REMOVER?

THIS ISN'T COMIN' OFF. I THOUGHT YOU SAID THIS COMES OFF WITH WATER.

IT DOES.

THEN WHY ISN'T IT COMIN' OFF?!

LOOKS LIKE THEY'RE HAVING SOME KIND OF PROBLEM.

WHAT THE—?

I HAVE RELATIVES COMING IN FROM ALL OVER, AND UNCLE M WON'T LET ME OUT OF THE HOUSE FOR FIVE MINUTES. NOT TO MENTION THE DANGER.

I NEVER THOUGHT OF IT THAT WAY.

I'D NEVER OPEN MY DOOR TO A STRANGER ON A NIGHT OF SUCH DARK POWER.

A NIGHT OF SUCH DARK POWER...

CHAPTER 4

SNORK

ETHAN!

ZZZ...

LENA?

UNCLE MACON! ETHAN! HELP!

YOU SAID I WAS SAFE HERE!

...!! RAVENWOOD!

THMP TMP

LENA!

ETHAN! HURRY! I CAN'T HOLD ON...

THE BOY PROTECTS HER. I'VE NEVER SEEN ANYTHING LIKE IT. NO CASTER CAN COME BETWEEN THEM.

BUT SARAFINE'S POWERS ARE GROWING BY THE DAY.

WE CAN'T STOP HER FROM COMING FOR LENA.

SLUMP

striking us

AFTER HALLOWEEN...

YOUR HOUSE WAS FULL OF THESE CREEPY PEOPLE WHO LOOKED LIKE THEY WERE AT A COSTUME PARTY.

HEH.

AND THEN YOU FOUND ME? YOU RODE IN ON YOUR WHITE STALLION AND SAVED ME?

DON'T JOKE. IT WAS REALLY SCARY. AND THERE WAS NO STALLION, IT WAS MORE LIKE A DOG.

...IT FELT LIKE THE CALM AFTER THE STORM. WE SETTLED INTO A ROUTINE, BUT...

...WE KNEW THE CLOCK WAS TICKING.

NO SIGNS OF FLIRTY SIRENS.

NO UNEXPLAINED CATEGORY 3 STORMS.

THEN THE UNTHINKABLE HAPPENED.

FREEZE

I CAN'T MOVE.

EVERYONE FROZE!

ETHAN? ARE YOU ALL RIGHT?!

DID I DO THIS?

CAST A TIME BIND? NO, YOU DIDN'T DO THIS, CHILD.

Gasp

THE GREATS FIGURED IT WAS TIME WE HAD OURSELVES A TALK, WOMAN TO WOMAN. NOBODY CAN HEAR US NOW.

EXCEPT ME, I CAN HEAR.

ARE YOU A CASTER?

NO, I'M JUST A SEER.

Haha!

WIGGLE

HAHAHA

LENA?

...

CRASH

UNCLE MACON! WAKE UP! THE SUN'S DOWN, I KNOW YOU'RE NOT ASLEEP IN THERE!

THE SUN'S DOWN, I KNOW YOU'RE AWAKE!

BANG

BANG

HUH?

AN UNDERGROUND PASSAGE?!

FWOOF

I CAN'T WAIT!

TMP

LET'S GO...

LENA LOOKS LIKE SHE CAN ALREADY FEEL THE MAGIC OF THIS PLACE.

WHAT I WAS FEELING WAS LESS MAGICAL.

THE BOOK OF MOONS HAS BEEN MISSING FOR OVER A HUNDRED YEARS...

ON MONDAY, LINK AND I PICKED LENA UP AT THE FORK IN THE ROAD. LINK LIKED LENA, BUT THERE'S NO WAY THAT HE'S GOING TO DRIVE RIGHT UP TO RAVENWOOD MANOR. IT'S STILL A HAUNTED MANSION TO HIM.

IF HE ONLY KNEW.

BUT ACCORDING TO LINK, THERE WAS TROUBLE OF ANOTHER KIND BREWING. HIS MOM HAD BEEN WHISPERING ON THE PHONE FOR THE PAST TWENTY-FOUR HOURS. WHEN LINK LISTENED IN, HE DIDN'T CATCH MUCH, BUT IT WAS ENOUGH TO FIGURE OUT HIS MOM'S END GAME.

"WE'LL GET HER OUTTA OUR SCHOOL, ONE WAY OR ANOTHER."

AND HER LITTLE DOG TOO.

SO, WHEN ARE YOU GONNA WRITE ME A SONG?

HaHa

RIGHT AFTER I FINISH THE ONE I'M WRITING FOR BOB DYLAN.

HOLY CRAP.

?

FREEZE

BLUE

NOW THERE'S A TERRIFYING SIGHT.

MY MOM!

DECEMBER MEANS ONLY ONE THING AT JACKSON HIGH: THE WINTER FORMAL.

IT WAS PRETTY OBVIOUS LENA WANTED TO BE ASKED. IT WAS LIKE SHE HAD A LIST OF ALL THE THINGS SHE IMAGINED A REGULAR GIRL WAS SUPPOSED TO DO IN HIGH SCHOOL, AND SHE WAS DETERMINED TO DO THEM.

THIS IS MY YEAR. I CAN FEEL IT. I'M GONNA GET SNOW KING THIS YEAR.

WHAT IS THAT, LIKE AN AFTER-SCHOOL SPECIAL?

YOUR GIRLFRIEND THINKS THAT I'M SPECIAL, DUDE.

IS THAT WHAT I AM?

IS THAT WHAT YOU WANT TO BE?

ARE YOU ASKING ME SOMETHING?

I GUESS I AM.

JUST LIKE THAT, I NOT ONLY HAVE A DATE TO THE WINTER FORMAL, I HAVE A GIRLFRIEND.

AND NOT JUST A GIRLFRIEND. FOR THE FIRST TIME IN MY LIFE, I ALMOST USED THE "L" WORD.

WHAT IF THE BOOK OF MOONS IS BURIED SOMEWHERE?

MAYBE WITH THE PERSON WHO UNDERSTOOD ITS POWER BETTER THAN ANYONE.

LENA! I THINK I KNOW WHERE THE BOOK IS!

I THINK IT'S WITH GENEVIEVE.

GENEVIEVE IS DEAD.

I KNOW.

WHAT ARE YOU SAYING, ETHAN?

I THINK YOU KNOW WHAT I'M SAYING.

CHAPTER 5

TRY NOT TO LOOK AT HER... SHE KEEPS STARING AT US WITH THOSE VACANT GOLD EYES...

CREEPY...

DIGGING UP A GRAVE UNDER A FULL MOON...! THIS IS SCARY. NOT RAVENWOOD SCARY. OR RIDLEY-TRYING-TO-KILL-ME SCARY... THIS IS LIKE THE THOUGHT OF LOSING LENA.

PARALYZING FEAR.

GRP

SKFF

WHAT WAS I THINKING?!

SCRFF

You were trying to right a wrong.

Take it.

SHE WANTS US TO TAKE THE BOOK.

WE FOUND IT!

AND GENEVIEVE'S GONE.

OUCH!

THUMP

IT BURNS!!

WHAT PART OF "ONLY A CASTER CAN TOUCH THIS BOOK" AREN'T YOU GETTING?

RIGHT. THAT PART.

EVERY TIME I TOUCH IT, MY HANDS BURN. IT'S LIKE WHEN I TOUCH LENA AND FEEL AN ELECTRIC SHOCK.

BUT WORSE.

HUNDREDS OF CASTS IN ENGLISH, LATIN, GAELIC, AND OTHER LANGUAGES...

DOES ANY OF THIS MEAN ANYTHING TO YOU?

NO. IN MY FAMILY, BEFORE YOUR CLAIMING YOU AREN'T REALLY ALLOWED TO KNOW ANYTHING.

IN CASE YOU GO DARK...

...I GUESS.

THESE PAGES ARE IN ENGLISH. SOMEONE STARTED TO TRASLATE IT IN THE BACK.

THE CLAYMING, ONCE BOUND, CANNOT BE UNBOUND. THE CHOICE, ONCE CAST, CANNOT BE RECAST. A PERSON OF POWERE FALLES INTO THE GREAT DARKENING OR THE GREAT LIGHT, FOR ALL TYME. IF TYME PASSES AND THE LASTE HOURE OF THE SIXTEENTHE MOONE FLEES UNBOUND, THE ORDER OF THINGS IS UNDONE. THIS MUST NOT BE. THE BOOKE WILLE BINDE THAT WHICHE IS UNBOUND FOR ALL TYME.

SO THERE'S REALLY NO GETTING AROUND THIS CLAIMING THING?

THAT'S WHAT I'VE BEEN TELLING YOU.

I'M NOT WORRIED.

ME NEITHER.

HA-HA-HA!

AT LEAST THE WINTER FORMAL MIGHT DISTRACT US A LITTLE...

IT'S BEAUTIFUL!

WHAT IF SHE'S SOME KIND OF PSYCHO?!

YOU THINK SHE'LL TIE ME UP OR SOMETHIN'?

HE'S UNDER HER SPELL ALREADY. IT DOESN'T MATTER WHAT I SAY...

LET'S DANCE!

LENA...

LET'S GET OUR PHOTO TAKEN.

TRY NOT TO WORRY ABOUT THEM...

FLASH

NEXT!

SPLASH

FLASH

AH!

RUINED.

I FELT SORRY FOR WHOEVER THEY WOULD BLAME FOR THIS MESS...

BUT OF COURSE—

AFTERWARD, I HEARD...

...MRS. LINCOLN FOUND SOMEONE TO BLAME.

THAT RAVENWOOD GIRL!

IT'S...INSANE.

HOW COULD MRS. LINCOLN BLAME LENA?!

WHY DOES SHE HAVE IT IN FOR HER?!

SHE PULLED THE FIRE ALARM AND DESTROYED EVERYTHING!

54 DAYS LEFT.

"AMONGST PERSONNES OF POWERE, THERE BEING TWINNE FORCES FROM WHYCHE SPRING ALL MAGICK, THE DARKNESSE AND THE LIGHT."

YOU THINK WE CAN SKIP TO THE GOOD PART? LIKE, LOOPHOLES FOR YOUR CLAIMING DAY?

IT GETS REALLY COMPLICATED. I'M NOT SURE I UNDERSTAND...

LENA...

SHE SHUT ME OUT.
I CAN'T HEAR HER
THOUGHTS OR TALK
TO HER...

HEY,
MAN.

I GOT A
FAVOR TO
ASK YOU.

SURE.

DECEMBER 23

THERE WAS SOMETHING IN THE AIR.

THE CLOSER IT GOT TO LENA'S BIRTHDAY, THE MORE I FELT IT.

DECEMBER 25

JANUARY 1

JANUARY 15

AT NIGHT WE STAYED UP LATE TALKING.

JANUARY 30

EVERY NIGHT SEEMED CLOSER TO THE NIGHT THAT COULD BE OUR LAST.

FEBRUARY 4

ONE DAY LEFT.

TWENTY-FOUR HOURS AND COUNTING.

NO MATTER HOW HARD WE TRIED, WE COULDN'T FIND ANYTHING IN THE BOOK OF MOONS.

CLIK

NOW WHAT?

SO, I HEAR IT'S LENA'S BIRTHDAY TOMORROW.

RIDLEY TOLD ME.

YOU TWO ARE STILL HANGING OUT?

TATTOO?!

I GOT IT OVER CHRISTMAS BREAK. PRETTY COOL, HUH? RIDLEY DREW IT HERSELF.

SHE'S A KILLER ARTIST!

YEAH, MAN. CAN YOU KEEP A SECRET?

HAVEN'T I ALWAYS?

EVEN THOUGH WE NEVER FOUND ANYTHING, I BETTER BRING THE BOOK.

SHFF

WHAT?

THE BOOK OF MOONS...

...OUR BOOK...

...IS GONE.

TODAY OF ALL DAYS!!

CHAPTER 6

Sixteen moons, sixteen years
Sixteen of your deepest fears
Sixteen times you dreamed my tears
Falling, falling through the years...

Sixteen moons, sixteen years
Sound of thunder in your ears
Sixteen miles before she nears
Sixteen seeks what sixteen fears...

Sixteen moons, sixteen years
Sixteen times you dreamed my fears,
Sixteen will try to Bind the spheres,
Sixteen screams but just one hears...

Sixteen moons, sixteen years
The Claiming moon, the hour nears,
In these pages Darkness clears,
Powers Bind what fire sears...

Sixteenth Moon, Sixteenth Year
Now has come the day you fear,
Claim or be Claimed,
Shed blood, shed tear,
Moon or Sun—destroy, revere...

RUSTLE

OH...

OH YEAH, THIS IS POSSIBLY THE ONLY PRESENT LENA IS GETTING TODAY.

GRAB

ETHAN, I LOVE IT!

IT BELONGED TO MY MOM.

ARE YOU SURE ABOUT THIS?

LENA KNOWS HOW I FEEL ABOUT MY MOM.

THIS IS A BIG DEAL.

I'M SURE... BECAUSE YOU'RE REALLY SPECIAL TO ME.

HOW SPECIAL?

IT REALLY FEELS LIKE ELECTRICITY.

WHEN WE KISS LIKE THIS, IT ALMOST HURTS.

Loneliness is holding the one you love ... when you know you might never hold him again.

WE STAYED IN HER ROOM
AS LONG AS WE COULD.
LENA DIDN'T WANT TO GO
DOWNSTAIRS.

BUT...

...MACON KEPT
CALLING UP
TO HER. WE
COULDN'T AVOID
IT FOREVER.

I GUESS WE
HAVE TO GO DOWN
THERE AND SEE
MY FAMILY.

WHAT...?

ETHAN, ARE YOU OKAY?

MY DAD IS...

ETHAN, DID YOU HEAR ME?

B...BUT... I CAN'T LEAVE LENA ALONE...

COME ON, MAN!

ETHAN!

......! LARKIN!

?

I NEED YOU TO TAKE LENA BACK TO THE HOUSE!

...?
SURE, MAN. I'LL TAKE HER BACK NOW.

I ALREADY LOST MY MOM... I KNOW MY DAD IS CRAZY, BUT I LOVE HIM. I CAN'T LOSE HIM TOO...!

DIDN'T YOU HEAR WHAT YOUR FRIEND SAID? I'M A WITCH. A BAD ONE.

THAT LOOK ON HIS FACE. THIS IS PROBABLY THE FIRST TIME LINK IS REALLY SEEING HER.

BUT YOU AREN'T ALL BAD. I KNOW THAT. WE'VE SHARED THINGS.

GASP

THAT WAS THE PLAN, HOT ROD. I NEEDED AN IN.

SO I COULD STAY CLOSE TO LENA.

I DON'T BELIEVE YOU...

LINK...WHATEVER SPELL RIDLEY CAST, HIS FEELINGS FOR HER ARE BIGGER THAN THAT.

WHAT ABOUT EVERYTHING YOU TOLD ME ABOUT YOU AND LENA GROWIN' UP TOGETHER?

WHY WOULD YOU WANT TO HURT HER?

LIKE I SAID, THIS IS MY JOB. GET ETHAN AWAY FROM LENA. THIS OLD GUY WAS JUST AN EASY TARGET.

HIS MIND IS WEAK.

"GET ETHAN AWAY FROM LENA."

THAT'S WHAT THIS IS ABOUT?

RID, DON'T DO IT!

DAD!

WHAT IS HE SAYING?? I CAN'T HEAR.

......

SHFF

NO, WAIT. THAT'S NOT MRS. LINCOLN.

CHAPTER 7

KNOW WHAT?!

YOUR UNCLE DIDN'T TELL YOU.

YOU AND ETHAN CAN NEVER BE TOGETHER, NOT PHYSICALLY.

CASTERS AND LILUM CANNOT BE WITH MORTALS.

AT LEAST NOT WITHOUT KILLING THEM.

CASTERS CANNOT BE WITH MORTALS WITHOUT KILLING THEM.

YOU CAN NEVER MARRY, NEVER HAVE CHILDREN. YOU CAN NEVER HAVE A FUTURE.

NO... THAT'S WHY THERE'S THAT ELECTRICITY WHENEVER WE TOUCH?!

I NEVER REALIZED HOW STRONG MACON IS...THAT TREE SNAPPED IN HALF!

...I CAN'T SEE ANYONE IN THIS SMOKE!

NOT HUNTING, LARKIN, SARAFINE... LENA...!

ETHAN! I'M UP HERE.

ON TOP OF THE CRYPT. BUT I THINK I'M STUCK.

HOLD ON, L. I'M COMING.

COUGH

WHAT?

INSIDE THE CRYPT.

THE BOOK OF MOONS?!

11:59 P.M.

LET HER
TRY TO STAY
LIGHT NOW.

EVERYTHING IS...
FROZEN.

......
......

ETHAN,
I LOVE YOU.
DON'T
LEAVE ME!!

THE
WORDS...

THE WORDS
FROM THE
VISIONS!

CHAPTER 8

I'M NOT GOING ANYWHERE.

AND NEITHER ARE YOU.

LENA TOLD ME WHAT
HAD HAPPENED WHILE I
WAS PASSED OUT...

MACON WAS THE ONLY
CASUALTY. APPARENTLY,
HUNTING OVERPOWERED
HIM AFTER I LOST
CONSCIOUSNESS.

MACON ALWAYS
SAID HE WOULD
DO ANYTHING FOR
LENA. HE WAS A
MAN OF HIS WORD.

AND SARAFINE...

I'M FUZZY ON THE
DETAILS, BUT LENA SOMEHOW
MANAGED TO BLOCK OUT THE
MOON AND SAVE HERSELF
FROM BEING CLAIMED.

WITHOUT THE CLAIMING,
IT LOOKS LIKE SARAFINE,
HUNTING, AND LARKIN FLED,
AT LEAST FOR NOW.

AND THEN THERE'S ME.
I GUESS I FELL WHILE
CLIMBING THAT CRYPT AND
KNOCKED MYSELF OUT.

LIKE AN IDIOT.

ONE EYE IS GREEN.

AND THE OTHER IS...GOLD.

......

CRNCH

DON'T
LET GO.

NEVER.

AUNT DEL OFFERED
TO DRIVE ME HOME, BUT
I WANTED TO WALK.

I NEED TO
CLEAR MY HEAD...

I STILL CAN'T
BELIEVE WE LOST
MACON.

THE RIGHT THING
AND THE EASY THING
ARE NEVER THE SAME.
NO ONE KNEW THAT
BETTER THAN MACON.

A NEW SONG?

Seventeen moons, seventeen years.
Eyes where Dark or Light appears.
Gold for yes and Green for no.
Seventeen the last to know.

THE END

BEAUTIFUL CREATURES:

THE MANGA

KAMI GARCIA & MARGARET STOHL

CASSANDRA JEAN

Adaptation and Illustration:
Cassandra Jean

Lettering: Abigail Blackman

BEAUTIFUL CREATURES: THE MANGA
Text copyright © 2009 by Kami Garcia and Margaret Stohl
Illustrations © 2013 Hachette Book Group, Inc.

Yen Press
Hachette Book Group
237 Park Avenue, New York, NY 10017

www.HachetteBookGroup.com
www.YenPress.com

Yen Press is an imprint of Hachette Book Group, Inc.
The Yen Press name and logo are trademarks of Hachette Book Group, Inc.

First Yen Press Edition: February 2013

ISBN: 978-0-316-18271-3

10 9 8 7 6 5 4 3 2 1

BVG

Printed in the United States of America